The Cleansing of the Knife

Of the seventy books by Naomi Mitchison the following are still in print:

Small Talk
All Change Here
To the Chapel Perilous
When the Bough Breaks
Memoirs of a Space Woman
Solution Three

FOR CHILDREN

The Family at Ditlabeng
Snake
The Big House

NAOMI MITCHISON

THE CLEANSING OF THE KNIFE

and other poems

CANONGATE
Edinburgh and Vancouver
1978

First published in 1978
by Canongate Publishing Limited,
17 Jeffrey Street, Edinburgh,
Scotland.

ISBN 0 903937 34 4

The publishers acknowledge the financial assistance of the Scottish Arts Council in the publication of this volume.

Printed by Thomson Litho Ltd,
East Kilbride Scotland.

Contents

A few of the poems included in this volume have already been published in *The Glasgow Herald* and *The Scotsman*.

The House of the Hare

At the time I was four years old
I went to glean with the women,
Working the way they told;
My eyes were blue like blue-bells,
Lighter than oats my hair;
I came from the house of the Haldanes
Of work and thinking and prayer
To the God who is crowned with thorn,
The friend of the Boar and the Bear,
But oh when I went from there,
In the corn, in the corn, in the corn,
I was married young to a hare!

We went to kirk on the Sunday
And the Haldanes did not see
That a Haldane had been born
To run from the Boar and the Bear,
And the thing had happened to me
The day that I went with the gleaners,
The day that I built the corn-house,
That is not built with prayer.
For oh I was clean set free,
In the corn, in the corn, in the corn,
I had lived three days with the hare!

The Alban Goes Out: 1939

Over at Arran the herring were good last night;
We cross Kilbrennan Sound in the tail of the day light,
The diesel going steady, the nets lying ready,
The Alban redded for working: that is our right.
And our neighbour boat, yon, within hail and sight.

You stand beside me, rocking as the boat rocks,
From the accustomed ankles, the knees in the grey
    rubber thigh-boots,
The swaying hips, dancer, oh dancer to the sea's moving,
    not mine now.
You hold the end of thirty fathom of wire
Dithering continuously to the water's tugging,
    and jerking
At the hand that waits to feel the definite patter,
Not the hard tap of mackerel, not a single fish
    nor a scatter,
But the feel of the whole herring shoal,
    oh a different matter:
The shoal you see flash on dark nights as you lie,
    intent, in the bows,
You can hear jump in a calm, or even smell,
Using all senses to fish the herring well.

The wind freshens, blowing off Arran, to a jabble of sea,
Away over Cour the sunset flames out into lovely ashes,
Embers of cloud floating on a clear farness.
A whale breaks and blows, three times, across our bows,
Smoothly like the rim of a black enormous wheel,
    emerging and turning.

Lights in Pirnmill, lights far astern in Carradale;
Supper in the boarding houses, fried eggs, new cake.

They have cards and whiskey and wireless, papers that
came with the mail.
But we are out all night with our living to make.
Them speaking of us, maybe, letting on our life's
the best:
Going out in the boats one night, making it into a tale!
Put you the kettle on, we'll be as good as the rest.

It is cozy down here, with the wee stove and the
strong smell of tea,
The cut bread and the jam, the talk and jokes on
the fishing,
Or some nights on the women, and all a man could
be wishing;
We will get in awhile from the sound and sight
of the sea.

The moon rises over Arran, creating immediately
The diamond path, older than all ancient roads.
Small lights come out, so many in the one darkness:
The orderly light-houses blink, up and down the coast,
And the Carradale fleet lights up.
Has Willie had a shot yet, or Robbie?
Not yet, not yet.

We lie about easy, after the tea, in our oil-skins,
Watching the moon break through,
Gossiping quietly, speaking of market prices,
Only the cruising engine and Sandy at the wheel,
Aware of what to do.

MacAllister comes from Grogport, goes back every day,
Five miles by the glen road, up Brackley way,
Past the big house, the Doctor's and the turn at
Campbell's shop,

The bright loops of the Carra, the green wood
of Croc,
By Brackley where the blackbirds are singing
between the rain,
And sweeter voiced than blackbirds, Jemima MacLean.

Oh Jemima's not for him, and Jemima's not for me,
Put me on your quota, lass, it's merry I would be!
It's I'd know how to please and it's I'd know
how to choose,
But MacAllister found a salmon once, and
no-one knows whose!

All at once the light,
The neighbour boat's light,
Winks, signals to us.
Alec has shot. Steady now.

They break out of dreams and gossip, run to
their places,
John Ritchie has the boat-hook, kneels, watches,
smiling, intent,
As Sandy steers for the dropped end of the ring-net
And the winkie, the tiny lamp,
Bobs on the jabble, hard to spear as a salmon.
John Ritchie has it!

Circling uptide, the ring-net surrounds the herring;
Both boats have their wheel-house lights to show that
they have shot,
For the fleet is close now, shouting from deck to deck,
Robbie has shot, MacBride has shot, have a care, man,
The nets is easy torn!

There are other trades, in the towns, where a man
would be glad,

Eyeing his neighbour, if business there was bad.
He must claw at his neighbour's throat like dogs that
fight in the street
But all that thought should be far from us in the
Carradale fleet.

We are working all the season, boat near to
boat in the nights,
And danger may come on us quick, no time to
stand upon rights.
When all our hands are as net-cut, and our eyes
as sore from the spray,
How can we think of our neighbours except
in a neighbourly way?

The circle closes,
To the neighbour boat;
We do not know
How many herring.
With sea and shouts,
With a great smacking,
Gunwale on fender,
We board, we board her.

The Viking shield-shape
Of the starboard tyres
On the boarded boat,
The Viking noises
Of the men who board her,
The single glare
Of the working light
On oil-skin armour,
On quick limbs heaving
In a battle turmoil,
The black-winged Valkyrs
With screaming babble

Of snatch and death,
Swoop to the circle,
That lights them up
As common gulls
Greedy for herring:
And the men not angry
But wise and working.

The Alban stands away now, rocking and dark,
Sandy alone aboard, in the wheel-house, keeping
The engine slow but a constant strain on the tow-rope
Between boat and boat, and so on the net, lest, slack,
The herring escape it. And he watches, across on
    the lighted Amy,
His four sons hauling at the net; Colin and Dick
    and Bob and Alec:
A share each for the house and a heart-lift for a father.

Men and engines grunting and hauling,
The nets dripping, the folds falling;
The spring-ropes jerking to the winches' creaking
Wind in by fathoms from their sea-deep seeking,
Steady and long like a preacher speaking.
But the flow of the net we must all lay hold on,
The cork-strung back-rope our hands are cold on.
As we thrash at the net the dead fish falling
Gleam and break from the tight mesh mauling,
Show what we'll get from the bag of the net!
And fierce and straining and shoulders paining
We drag it out from the sea's wild sprawling,
From the lit wet hummocks' twist and spin;
And the leaded sole-rope comes slumping in.

The bulging net
Between Alban and Amy,
Plenty good herring,

Pass the riddle,
Thirty baskets and maybe more!
Wind and wet
And the two boats jogging,
Mind your hand now!
Fend her off, boys!
There was the way the old net tore.
Pull out the net,
They're into the riddle,
The wee ones swimming
To dark and safety for another year.
Wind and wet,
Down with the basket,
Haul them up, lads!
Into the hold now.
There's a week of expenses clear!
Sleep and sweat
And we rub our faces.
It's after midnight.

Fine fat herring, good to be seen,
Blue and pink and silver and green,
Tinsel bellies and strong backs brown;
They flip like fleas as we shovel them down.
Easy to ask and hard to tell
If the dark of the hold is the herrings' hell.

Green to green and red to red—
How can we tell our neighbour boat?
Over wet dark acres the lights are shed,
The moon is hidden, the clouds are high,
Thirty couple that shift and float.
But a wife can tell her man in the bed
By little touchings of hand or thigh,

And so we tell our neighbour boat
By the slope of her lights in the blink of an eye—
Perfect safety, go ahead.

Sleepy, sleepy, the night goes by,
And up and down goes the Carradale fleet,
Seeking and silent or shouts for a shot;
With here a winkie, half dark, half-bright,
As the neighbour boat steers hard for the light;
And there a mile of shadow and water
And an echo of knocking, wise or not.
(Is it black enough for the fire in the water,
The burn of the herring that dart from the knocking,
The jar of the knock of mallet on gunwale
That shivers the water?—the rocking, jogging
Field of water, unploughed, unsowed.)
And dark the land as an anchored ship,
And warm and cozy lie he and she,
Asleep in their beds, as we would be.
And only a head-lamp's twist and dip
Of one late car on the Crossaig road.

But the moon rides up, too clear for the burning,
And John has the wire and Sandy's steering
Towards Skipness Point like a slow hound turning.
And away on the Amy the decks are clearing,
Tea's in the fo'csle, hot and cheering.
And along the port quarter, laid and plain,
The nets are redded for work again.

Sloan alone at the end of the Sound,
Canniest fisher of all the Clyde,
First in the market, many's the pound
Comes in to Sloan at the Ayr quay-side.

If we ask for his luck, would he tell or show?
Who are his friends and what's his plan?
But now we're up to a boat we know,
And now we shout for a Carradale man.

You kneel on the rocking deck
And the two boats kiss,
As the two brother skippers,
Fine and handy at this,
Bring them alongside gently,
Calling the news to each other:
Little there is to miss!
And the waves tumble and shove
At the Alban and Cluaran,
And sometimes your face is below me,
And sometimes above.

I have seen you kilted and fine
Like a laird and all at the Mod,
But it's oil-skins now and an odd
Hat that's been out all weathers
And more at sea than on land;
And the hand on the gunwale by mine
Is a grimed and working hand.
And though you have seen no herring,
It's Gosh, aye, bonny!
Because of the night and of friendship
That's easy to understand.

It will be morning soon;
Down slides the moon to setting and the stars tremble;
Dawn will come up over Arran.
But there is time yet, there is time
For the morning herring.
The wind drops, and the diesel ticking over
Quiets all pulses.

Dreams, moony, slide between one word and the next;
Standing, we sleep.

But the wire speaks suddenly: now, now,
To the net, boys!
And the winkie goes overboard and we pay her out
By folded fathoms, quickly and carefully,
To windward of the herring,
And Sandy steers in the great circle of catching
And flicks his mast-head light.

Morning herring,
Best in the market,
No great haul but
It's morning herring:
Ten bob a basket
And eight to share,
With boats' share, net's share and engine's share:
Fifty baskets
And it's us for Ayr!

The Alban sets for Ayr and the Amy sets for home,
And the Cruban light ahead welcomes the Carradale boats:
We have been out all night, mother,
    we will no longer roam...
And the grey dawn will show us our point of
    the wild white goats.

And neat as a woman's kitchen, the Amy is redded up;
Bob yawns and stretches, and Blue has a snatch of sleep;
Charley has rinsed the teapot and put by every cup;
And a porpoise sighs and sneezes
    like a queer old man of the deep.

And it's easy steering for Alec,
    with the light lifting fast,

And he throws the broken herring out for a moment's play
Where the gulls scramble and chatter,
    crowding along by the mast,
And a fine gannet among them, that's wakened for the day.
A bonny bird is the gannet; he goes the fisherman's way.

The wind drops. Smoothly, steadily,
Without difficulty arriving
On the half tide at Port Crannaig,
The pier, empty and dejected,
Waits for our making fast.
On the cold edge of morning
The Carradale houses sleep.

Going up from the harbour,
It is too light for ghosts,
Too early for land folk.
Sandy is at Ayr or near; Dick and the rest,
Donald MacAllister, John Ritchie and Colin.
Alec has berthed the Amy;
They will be sleeping soon,
Sound sleeping when the summer visitors
Blink over breakfast at the summer sun.
The Cluaran is out yet, and the Mairi Bhan;
Others are heading for home:
Queen of the Fleet, Water Cress, Maid of Honour,
Thalassa, Polly Cook...

At Airds I smell new bread; there is a light in the bakehouse.
As I pass in the dawn the smell grows so rich that it covers
The smell of herring on my coat and hands.
It dies along the road and instead I smell,
As the first gold comes breaking through the grey,
All the land things; earth, flowers, cattle, houses
Where the goodwife begins to stir,
And, under the high green arches between gate and doorway,
The essential sweetness of leaves.

The Scottish Renaissance in Glasgow: 1935

This city, builded on more hills than Rome was,
With a river bigger than Tiber, tidal and foamless,
I came to in the cold winter of a bad trade year,
I, Scottish too, with the same hunger for knowledge laden.
Somewhere in all this bareness, these squared, grey houses
Of harsh, unweathering stone, only ill thoughts rousing,
Somewhere up grim stairs,
        steep streets of fog-greased cobbles,
In harsh, empty closes with only a dog or a child sobbing,
Somewhere among unrhythmic,
        shattering noises of tram-ways
Or by cranes and dock-yards, steel clanging and slamming,
Somewhere without colour, without beauty,
        without sunlight,
Amongst this cautious people,
        some unhappy and some hungry,
There is a thing being born as it was
        born once in Florence:
So that a man, fearful, may find his mind fixed on tomorrow.
And tomorrow is strange for him, aye,
        full of tearings and breakings,
And to the very middle he feels his whole spirit shaken.
But he goes on.

Adoption of a Parliamentary Candidate, Lochgilphead: 1939

We are beginning to make something
That was not here before.
I will be true to you.
Or maybe that was here once
But died and must rise again.

I would die for you if it comes to that.
We are plain folk here, we work with our hands, most of us.
We have been at the fishing; We have been lifting potatoes;
we have been
Driving lorries. We want sense from you, not death: life.
I will live for you then.
Sense is what we need, a world of each for all, a world
Where we can live kindly by one another, without
greed or hate,
Where men and women are no more wasted,
nor work in vain.
I will try to make your world.
We are come together for this. In a small town,
in a small way,
Over strong tea and scones we have decided.
You are our man.
It may be something will come of this beyond what we dream.
I give myself to you.
You shall be worked hard. You must help us and stand by us,
Compose our quarrels, go over our balance sheets,
find out the law for us.
You will get us a rise in wages.
I will be proud to serve you.
We will worry you, suck your heart's blood, we will take
your rest from you,
Come between you and your girl's lips
or the page of the book you are reading.
Ah, my friends, I do not think of that now!
Will you have me?
Yes, we will have you, Comrade.

The War Experience

The Farm Woman: 1942

Why the blue bruises high up on your thigh,
On your right breast and both knees?
Did you get them in the hay in a sweet smother of cries,
Did he tease you and at last please,
With all he had to show?
Oh no, oh no,
Said the farm woman:
But I bruise easy.

Why the scratched hand, was it too sharp a grip,
Buckle or badge or maybe nail,
From one coming quick from camp or ship,
Kissing as hard as hail
That pits deep the soft snow?
Oh no, oh no,
Said the farm woman:
But I bruise easy.

There was nothing, my sorrow, nothing that need be hidden,
But the heavy dung fork slipped in my hand,
I fell against the half-filled cart at the midden;
We were going out to the land.
Nobody had to know.
And so, and so,
Said the farm woman:
For I bruise easy.

The tractor is ill to start, a great heaving and jerking,
The gear lever jars through palm and bone,
But I saw in a film the Russian women working
On the land they had made their own,
And so, and so,
Said the farm woman:
And I bruise easy.

Never tell the men, they will only laugh and say
What use would a woman be!
But I read the war news through, every day;
It means my honour to me,
Making the crops to grow.
And so, and so,
Said the farm woman:
But I bruise easy.

The Farmer and her Cows

At the morning milking, what is the farmer thinking?—
Through the shiny green dawning driving her cows
That roll over and come slowly, snuffing and drinking,
With none else to wonder what the farmer allows.

A long day ahead now, the farmer is saying,
Tired I shall be, my cows, and glad of my bed;
Oh in the evening how I'll beat you for straying,
When the wet trees drip down rain on my head.

Lucky you, my cows, that can no way get knowing
The day of your calving, your bleeding, your pain:
On what lorry your calves to the slaughter house going
On a green shiny morning that turns back to rain.

The Burial of Elie Gras

Elie Gras, Elie Gras, we are coming towards you
Through the choking ring of the continuous bells,
Through our bare tears, wherein the sky is broken
As the heart is broken, breaking the sky,

Round the great evening bird whose eyes are ocean
Where burns your secret star, the star of death.

Elie Gras, Elie Gras, the birds are crying your name.
The sweeping, widowed seagulls cry and are lit
By the sudden sun-splash on the wide waves, crying,
Crying your name as the sea breaks, crying,
Your name, its salt crests broken on the rock-sharp wind.

The half-grown boys, thin and fair-haired, almost children,
With death in their glassy hearts, their eyes
　　sliding slowly
From the bottom of deep thoughts,
Used to watch street corners, roofs, shed-doors
　　cautiously opened:
Men pale as children with hearts of brushwood cover,
　　of smoke,
Yet clear in action as water over stones,
Used to follow you in the street fingering their
　　black guns:
Used to follow you, Elie Gras, the cartridge belt
　　over the heart,
And in the evening the tommy-guns
Twinkled, like a river's ripple, for you.

The half-grown boys with their starved hearts,
　　thin as the wind
On straw or water, the men simple and sad
With ploughmen's eyes, hands soaked in air of evening,
Eyes of the great roads, eyes—Oh, let us face reality!
Men who walked out of the bar to get to the fighting,
Quite simply, with grimy, ordinary clothes,
Men heavy with the dirt of the other war,
They went by.

Went by in front of the old men at the windows,
Whose eyes worn like the wooden handles of their old tools,
Watched the passing of the funeral procession,
The immense, the national obsequies
Of Elie Gras, Franc-Tireur,
Who died for France;
Died for the world, died
For earth and wine and girls, for the children and the
high-school,
Died for French history and the Marseillaise at the
back of it,
Died for mankind.

Yes, you are dead, you are dead.
No-one could be more dead than you,
Elie Gras, you, Elie Gras.
Yesterday even . . .
But we must take our misery up again,
Re-live it carefully, analysed, free of memories;
We must let it paint a circle of anger round us,
The flag-flap of a red flag, of a flag
Of sky and blood, to whose red your death adds,
The flag for which you died.
Yesterday, yesterday, even . . .

Elie, oh can't you hear us, Elie Gras?
You are asleep. No you are not asleep,
But dead, no-one could be more dead
Than Elie Gras, you, Elie Gras,
Covered with dust but coming clear of the dust
As a stone god that the wind sweeps away the dust from.

When they laid Elie Gras into the mothering earth,
Mother of winds and houses and children and the sky,
When they laid Elie Gras down in the slow currents of earth,
Forming and dissolving and Elie Gras returned to it,

When they yet waited, trembling and troubled,
Like the ripe corn under a change of wind,
When they left Elie Gras under the earth, along
As the root of a dead tree, they went away, they scattered
Out of the cemetery, beyond laws
And beyond the breaking of laws.

translated from the poem
by Diamant-Berger, killed 1944.

Then

The rainy, midgy, Highland morning
Comes on me as it came on my forefolk;
They could lie in their beds and blether;
I must get up and milk the cows,
I must go out to the autumn weather.

Oh the evenings of songs and dancing,
Brush of the kilt and touch of partners—
Dust on the pipes and the dancers dumb.
Now I twist the knob of my programme,
Cold as fairies the voices come.

1943

Bronzer than leaf green, see, the abrupt plover
Expands to a black bright, white flapping flower.
Tumultuous dice-board bird, tumbling, mad in Spring,
Bounced up from earth, down from clouds, to all winds crier,
Furl your self, flower, become bronze, stealthy, crested,
Watcher from pastures. Oh, watch a little, plover,
Nor be too glad this Spring.

Kintyre

Kintyre

I wake when the wind changes.
Beyond the dark Firth far,
Where the waves clap and the tides rustle
      and the herring are,
At the far side of the great Clyde the wind ranges.
I wake as it changes.

If snow flew or mist blew
East on the hills of Renfrew,
Here, Arran sheltered, we might never know,
Get no breath of sleet or hard snow,
Until across mountain ranges
The wind backs and changes.

Clear starlight as sleep takes me,
But a cloud creeps from the side.
My dream no more ranges
Through a universe at rest,
But quick through the window wide,
From Atlantic on the west
Or from east beyond Clyde,
Leaps anxious into my breast.
I wake when the wind changes.

On a Highland Farm

I wait in the fall of day
For the marauding deer
That tore my potato drills,
Rooting my good Kerr's Pink
And at dawn, like shadows, away,
The earth was scarred with the mark
Of the knife-hard hoofs of the stag,

Of the tall and the short hind.
But their shapes are ill to find
In the pressing, gathering dark,
And the twigs quiver and jag
On the thorn by which I hide,
And the sidling shadows bunch
And the wind comes with the tide,
And the storm-blown larches hunch
Like the crouched backs of dreams.
In a world made insecure
For me as for the deer,
Between a horror and lure
Where reason could be undone,
In a wood of wind and fear,
There exists only my gun,
My clever, my man-made gun.
All that is real to me,
To end what was begun
When the bad deer came to my crops,
Are the barrels and stock of my gun
And the knife against my knee.

Living in a Village

Living in a village is walking
Among snare wire, being
The bulge-eyed rabbit, ware of
The light heart, dancing gossip-stoats, the blood-lipped,
Biding their time.
Living in the Big House is being
The big stag, the twelve-pointer,
Watched on, edible, spied and lied to,

From burrows, runways, witch-twisted bushes, and most
From the hoodies' rock where the observant, the cautious,
    the hungry hoodies
Feed upon small game still, hoping for bigger,
And bide their time.

To a Fisherman with the Present of a Knife

When you cut the bread
Remember me
Who will be far
From ship and sea,
Whose books unread,
Whose heart unread,
Are like a star,
Remote, remote,
As such things are,
Far from your boat
A polar star.

Up Loch Fyne

The humped grey fish-watcher has become with one wing flap
The elegant trailing heron that Hokusai dreamed up,
Far from Loch Fyne.
May my own squat and spear-beaked mind
Fishing and gulping its needs among weedy statistics
Or in the dazzle of every-day reflections and refractions,
Sometimes take wing and re-create a myth.

THREE POEMS
(For the Highlands & Islands Advisory Panel)

I. Duncraig

The lochan, speckled
With rain-drops and rises,
The rush-thatched boat shed
And the two white horses.
Oh my love, you are far from home now.

The moss dripping
And the young ferns curly,
The late primrose
And the banks of rhodie.
Oh my love, you are far from home now.

Behind the clouds
Is the sun's self waiting,
But behind the bens
Is another ben
And behind sorrow
Is the mother of sorrows.
Oh my love, you are far from home now.

II. Raasay

My curse on age
And the limbs' ache,
The skirt hiding
A lie of ankles,
A knee no longer
Wanting the brush
Of a kilt swinging.
I looked for a thing but I could not find it.

My curse on age
And the head's knowledge
That comes too late
For the heart's help:
On the lie of laughter
And the red fuchsia
In the grey hair.
I looked for a thing but I could not find it.

III. Wester Ross

Stone and rock,
Boulder and pebble,
Water and stone,
Heather and stone,
Heather and water
And the bog cotton that is not for weaving.

Peats uncut
And the orange moss
Under sharp rush
And spiked deer-grass,
Under tough myrtle
And thin blue milkwort,
And ever, ever,
The silver shining
Of the bog cotton that is not flowers.

The stones drop
From the height of the bens,
In the low houses
Of the dead crofters
The rafters drop,
And the turf roof:

Stone after stone
The walls are dropping,
And the bog creeps nearer
With the bog cotton for the fairies' flag.

Later Poems

East Coast—West Coast

Belled and citied,
Her windy childhood
Slept with flag-stones
And dreamt with roof tops,
High and gritted.

Lull the birches
Her bird-swept aging,
Close and gardened.
Bulb and stolon
Her skilled hand searches,
Stills the raging
For wind and houses.

The Highland Scene: The Great Fault

There is a loch of tears with great monsters in it,
Though no-one believes in them but I who have seen them.
They come skulking and rippling through, minute by minute
Leaving the waters dark and disturbed between them.

Here stand reflected mountains of ancient guilt,
Half bare, half forested with witch-loved spruces.
Along their flanks a narrow road has been built,
From end to end trailing its own abuses.

But on the bright surface boats are constantly going,
For fish or trade, merry with the lock-keepers' daughters,
As Adam was merry with Eve under green leaves growing,
Forgetting what always lies under the deep water.

The Boar of Badenoch and the Sow of Athol

Few have seen the King Selkie and few the grand
Sweep of the wings as the Queen Swan comes to land,
In the long light days of summer when
florrish is sweet on the bough,
Seeking their island mates between the machair and plough.
But none saw the Boar of Badenoch cover his sow.

Away on the skerry the Selkie nurses his dream,
Far from her shining bridal the Swan has flown.
And the Boar of Badenoch couches, stiff and alone,
Weighted, the ridge of his bristles,
with scree and heather and stream
For his sow has eaten her pigs and turned into stone.

Buachaille Etive Mor and Buachaille Etive Beag

Those two had shepherds, hunched above their sheep,
Dreaming of blood and pain and the long sleep
In their too certain circumstance of when:
Two black shepherds and myself and the Glen.

If you speak ill of the shepherds, speak it low;
Wait for the winter, they say, wait for the snow,
Wait for the night of the Campbells, the day of the fox,
The frayed rope and the boot that slips on the rocks.

Next Stop Perth

That was my place that I am far from.
Those were my hills I climbed all over.
Through that tunnel I went under
My now over-passing railway line.

That was my love I burned for the touch of.
That was my faith I worked and lived for.
In those dreams was pained foreknowledge
Of the chilling age-years that now are mine.

Those were my ghosts that I gave way to.
Now from within the shape of terror
I see me young and in frozen fear of
My fetch that is giving the counter-sign.

Early o

Early o, early in the morning town,
Bare stand I out of my sweaty night-gown;
I brush my teeth and my hair that is yet brown.

Early o, early in the morning air,
The bitch squats to pee against the outside stair;
My poor bones are aching: I ask you is it fair?

Early o, early in our morning state,
The cold smoke starts to trickle up from the grate;
Strong tea on the hob, bacon on the plate.

Early o, early as the morning breaks,
On the grey glass of Loch Tarbert the swan wakes;
The young must live and make their own mistakes;
The old must go, far, far, for all our sakes.

The Cleansing of the Knife
1941–1947

I. Why do we lift the glass?

The thoughts stream up from the knife
That lies under my head:
Dreams of you and your life
And the wish you have to be dead:
Blood, blood on the sgian.

I am a woman of Scotland,
I have read my history through,
Have turned to the last page,
Minding your like and you
With rising flames of rage,
As I think of you at Minard,
Escaping out of one cage
Into another cage.

Dark stand the centuries
Of ill days for the Highlands.
Tears in the glen, tears
For oppression of all kinds:
For the chief's targes and spears
As the stag goes by with his hinds,
And there's courage and song and laughter
And the plaids go swirling wide;
But the common man must hunt
For the black shells in the sea-weed
Between a tide and a tide.
They could get laughing and bleed you
As their kind has done since.
Though there were times you were free,
The like of Wallace could lead you,
You know the way he died,
The thing he was needing to face
Alone amongst the English.

We do not know what he thought,
Strapped and dragged on the hurdle,
On his way to the last place
And the worst pains he could get.
When we begin to think
Of the way they were killing Wallace,
We know we had best forget;
We lift the glass and we drink.

How will I make you hear
The echo out of your heart
Put into words of my own?—
Make action rise out of fear,
Strike land from a cold chart,
Grow flesh on an old bone?
I know now that I speak
With a voice not of mine,
Knowledge beyond books:
I speak with the voice of Scotland,
Alba our mother,
And the blooded knife her sign.
Will you dare to turn your face
Back to the common way
Of forgetting and disgrace?
Ah Highlander, son of Alba,
Will the glass seem so gay?

Tears in the glen, tears
And a blackness in the mind.
Watching the centuries:
Exile of every kind,
The foreign legions of Scotland.
Oh heart, heart of Bruce,
Bruce that died too soon,
We follow thee with a sore smart, reins loose,
Forby our much anger and pain,

Beyond France, beyond Spain,
Or the place of the full moon
In the hills behind the hills.
Far death there for squire and knight,
But the common man in the fight
Without bonny blade or ox-priced armour,
His the worst plight
And for his folk the worst ills.

Tears, tears in the glen
For the flower of them, the best,
My bonny lad, my bit lassie,
Gone, gone with the rest,
Leaving the kindly west
For Glasgow and beyond all my ken,
Far side of the long Clyde.
Will they come back again?
No need now of the double sight,
They are scattered as a blown stack
Through a long and wild night.
Tears will not bring them back.

Between Minard and Carradale
You will see the dark, squared walls,
Sheep-folds that tell an ill tale
Of ruined steading and byre,
Lost homes where once was loving and laughter.
But the folk went far from Kintyre
And the thatch came down with the rafter.
Landlord's doing, yon.
Are you angry, Donnachadh Bàn?
Nothing good happened after.
When we begin to think
Of the Highland clearances,
Of lairds and money and sheep,
We had best forget and drink
And the drink has need to be deep.

Tears in the glen, tears.
What is the use of writing
Stories and poems and songs?
The makars who are dead, and the old seers
Attacked all kinds of wrongs
In a gallant mocking and flyting,
Curses that would lift a log.
What good did all that do?
Could the songs change one Campbell,
Take one acre from Stair?
Burns died like a dog.
What song of his could alter
The presbytery of Ayr?
When he began to think
Of that theocracy,
He had to forget and drink.
Can it be otherwise
For folk like you and me?

Tears in the glen, tears
For the shock of terror by night,
The unexplainable fears
Of the bairn alone in her bed.
They have dowsed the friendly light,
The Mass, the carols, the Harvest Home,
Instead
The witch, the warning, the punishment, the Sight:
Hell-fire waits for all,
Mother cannot help or hear
The lost bairn's whimper and call
From the coals of eternity
Outwith heaven's hard wall.
Sermons have made it clear:
No act of ours, no love nor faith nor prayer
Can change predestined fate,
Lighten our muckle fear.

Thus only the Word saith:
The beginning was already too late.
Aye, draw no easy breath:
The luck comes three times and the third time death.
When we begin to think
Of ill luck and hell fire,
We are needing quick to stop.
We snatch the glass and we drink.

Tears in the glen, tears
For the things that were done to us,
For betrayal down the years
And we surprised and dumb,
Not seeing a way to do.
Fletcher of Saltoun knew
What the Union would make of us.
We tried to remain true
To too many lost causes.
But the ship sailed from the bay,
The Highlands were left to pay.
Time we learnt to betray:
We can sink behind ourselves
As one sinks behind a stone
And sharpens a knife on the sole.
The key turns soft in the lock
As we hide the thoughts in our head.
Or, if they must get loose,
There's an easy way to drown them,
To make ourselves one with the dead.
We need not begin to think
What oppression has made of us.
We can lift the glass and drink.

Tears in the glen yet, tears of shame.
We have been proud and kind,

Have given our food to strangers.
We had our own music,
Great music that a man could mind
And be glad of his race and name.
We do not sing that now.
Only the little music
That goes down well in the south,
Where they turn soft and jocose,
Over laid with sentiment
And the air-sick lewdness of cities.
Who now has the singing mouth
Fit for the great music?
Smoking and drinking spoils it,
We are not caring for that,
Nor who gets profit on bottle or packet.
Only another boss
Over our mountains and rivers, our sorrow, our loss,
Our shame. What pennies can we get back out of them?
Ach, turn about and drink!
Donnachadh Bàn, your boss too is in London
Dare you to wait or think?

Once it was water of life,
The bards were drinking it,
Sharpening all their senses.
It came from our own barley,
The scent of the heather was in it.
It would rust no knife.

When a thing is used for life
At fixed and life-giving seasons,
For a breaking of barriers
To the music all should play,
For good rhymes and good reasons,
Then it is water of life.
It is not that today.

II. What can we see?

Here is the problem set,
Demanding a clear head:
What can we do for Scotland?
The past that must not be forgotten
For all our wish to forget:
Ourselves in the stream of the dead,
Pushed on ahead of them
Through a night that shows no clearing,
To a future we cannot see
And if we did would be fearing.
They could not tell when they sowed,
What corn would spring from the seed.
Neither can we tell.
We can only know direction,
But not to where it may lead.
The Word may come to ourselves
As it came once to Knox,
A grievous and heavy load.

But if it speaks through us
Then we are Scots indeed.
Lay the close look on life,
Watching what folk have needed
And their descendants need.
Peer back as Scott did once
But clearer than ever he did,
Seeing our folk in bond
In a poor and a hard land,
But slowly getting freed
Through their own thought and sweat.
If we can help this to happen
Through times that are harder yet,
Then we are Scots indeed.

I ask you, Donnachadh Bàn,
Were you thinking of Scotland at all,
Or of any but yourself,
In a soft daze of self-pity
And self devoted tears:
Thinking of old days at Minard,
Other New Years,
Resolutions you have not kept,
Dreams brushed out by the day?
If we are Scots indeed
Such tears should not be wept,
We can make the break-away,
Leave other hearts to bleed
Over what's best forgotten,
Remember what we should
And let the lave go by,
Planning for Scotland's good.
Can we do it, Donnachadh Bàn?

III. Carradale to London: Blood promise

You say you will try to do it,
The pity it would be
For a poem to have no ending
You lay your hand by mine,
The red is scarring it still.
But a promise may go ill,
Words between you and me
And a break you cannot be mending.
There's a stronger cord to twine,
It is more than a promise I need,
More than a Highlander's promise:
Though we hope to be Scots indeed,
Though we note the hour and the minute

And the place of the soul's lending.
And ach, the spite would be in it
For my poem to have no ending!
Now I go south, to the war:
The sgian goes with me
I am not forgetting Scotland.
Here at my heart's core
Lie all of you, my friends.
Across wild land and sea
Love goes quicker than bombers
To its own mixing of ends.
Your wish for death and passion—
Deirdre, Mary Stuart
And the girls in the old songs—
Flares with my sense of life,
Of direction steadily kept
And a steady righting of wrongs
And a cleansing of the knife.
See yourself, Donnachadh Bàn,
And I will stand beside you;
In the cold morning mirror
I will let no phantoms ride you.

Friend, is this how you are,
Is this the man I know:
A Highlander and lonely,
Oppressed by historical causes,
Aware how things should be,
Not how to make them so?

And times you are feeling that only
Hate is the thing you can see,
Or to be like other men,
Disguised in their disguises.
You know the way to that,
As you know the shame that rises

Through the long Sunday morning,
That asks to be drowned again.

And a man can lie in his bed
Or a man can try to pray,
Stiff in his Sunday suit,
To a God who is far away,
No more the fountain of life.
But here is something instead
For us who are Scots and care
For the cleansing of the knife.
And maybe God is there,
Shaped as a new Word
At the very heart of our plan,
And hard for us to see,
Since God changes with man
And all man asks to be.

IV. What are you doing?

What are you doing today,
What doing tonight?
Do you see over Carradale Bay
Stars in a frosty height?
Are you a writer or reader
Or seeker for the dew-pearled rose?
Do you dream you are a leader
In some feud of the clans,
Mackenzies against Munros?
Foulis Castle all on flames!
Or are you working on plans,
Timber for sleepers and pit-props,
Or seedlings in even rows
With their bonny sounding names,
Grandis and nobilis?

Have you been out with the lorries?
Have you watched from Rhonnadale heights
The soft, slow changing of lights
Away over to Islay?
Have you planted with the double spade-cut
For generations to come?
Or have you been with friends,
Thinking in anger: yon woman,
Her from the Big House,
Why must she interfere?
Time that thing ends.
Empty the glass, let the bright whirl-pool hum
See: she will disappear!

Scotland will need to be led,
But never by one man only,
Of whatever wrongs a righter:
Not that for any excuse!
Those days are dead,
Dead with Wallace and Bruce.
Now no one talker and fighter,
But leaders here and there
With sense and honour and pride,
Men and women of Scotland
Through city and country-side,
Waking their fellows to think
And act as Scots indeed,
But aware of the danger's brink
For all who hope to lead.

V. Blitz on Clydebank 1941

Man, how is it you are?
Are you free and well?
Have you looked through hell gates
At the raw mouth of hell,
Have you brought your soul to the bar,
Saying: however I go
This will not be my choice?

I am thinking you will not tell,
Neither to me nor another,
Though once I spoke with the voice
And strength of Scotland our mother:
She that has need of the knife,
That speaks to blood and bone.
But a man's soul is his own
And his own his life,
Let him go to heaven or hell.
I need not be asking you
For I know you will not tell.

Where are you, Donnachadh Bàn,
And what way are you minded?
I cannot see you at all;
My eyes are blinded
By the grey plaster dust
Of a smashed house in Partick,
Where a boy's body lay
Smashed in with the plaster,
Day after aching day.
We act because we must
And I had need to be there.
Yet each is responsible
For the actions of a brother.
We cannot shift the weight

Of kindness or of care,
Nor is it ever too late
For one to stand by another.
I tried to stand by you:
As, now, I am thirled to trust
The kindness of my friends.
I know there is one thing true:
Even at most alone
We are more than merely ourselves;
Our souls are not our own.

The knife was with me in Glasgow,
The sgian turned to a sign:
Where hell's sign from the south-east
Had come in a new design
Of night and shock and death.
Will we face it, Donnachadh Bàn?
Show me your hand at least
To tell if the scar is on it!
The red still stays on mine;
But my hand was the whiter,
Mine was the laird's hand,
The cool hand of the writer.
I cannot see on your own,
It is scratched with briar and wire.
—What's one scar more or less?
Ah, leave the hand alone
And take your eyes from the life
Before you get my curse,
Woman from the Big House!—
God sent no sign to Clydebank.
There was death and fear and fire,
And the waiting that is worse,
That brings the grey to the hair.
But we who were here or there,

Drawers of dividends,
In the easy snarl of money
Either as wage or share,
Ourselves had made such things
The whole end of man.
We built the tenements
That crashed and crumbled to filth.
God was no part of the plan.
We must take the weight of the blame:
Clydeside is Scotland's shame
And was, before they came
With the death cross on their wings.
We begin to understand;
Our thoughts take words and shape.
Show me a hand or a thought,
Let me have my poem's ending!
But you keep your thought and your hand,
You slip away and escape
With the thing you are defending
From the woman who has known
All that is ill to mind:
Things that no-one should know.
And a man's soul is his own;
You will neither tell nor show.

If you have chosen for Scotland
There is no easy way
Either of thinking or living.
Ah, Highlander, our ways are blocked:
Old ways of loving and giving,
The clear light of the day
On the hillside and the deer running,
The fine point of honour,
The clean blade of the sword.
We must have the serpent's cunning
To deal with money and power.

To endure and twist and break
And bind with a strong cord:
Since there may yet, man, come an hour
That the cities cannot take,
Not having the way of it.
That will be our time,
We will have the say of it,
If our hands and heads are clear.
Your hand will be on the knife,
My own is bound to be near:
The uncleansed knife of Scotland
That will be bright at last.
For our souls are not our own,
We are held by future and past
And the love and care of our friends.
We cannot be alone.

VI. Shifting the Sand

With war and work and farming,
Day's darg, the months pass.
From end to end of the Bay
The storms have shifted the sand
And thrown the wrack on the grass.
Your mind is turned away,
With stress of work and of war;
More wood at the saw-mill,
More acres to me
Between the road and the shore,
And a book I am needing to write
When a long seuch like the sea
Stirs the thing to be born,
And the words wake me at night.
I have harrowed my fields with horses,
I have sown my own corn,

Snedded my own turnips,
Mastered my own fears.
The soc of the plough drives under
Turf that is matted with years:
Does the soc drive too deep?
Does it drive too deep for Scotland?
The storms have shifted the sand
And Scotland stirs in her sleep;
I have planned and written for Scotland.
But a working farmer's hand
Is scarred with thorns and snedders.
What's one scar more or less
From a knife that's used on wood,
On tarred string and for skinning,
Or to scrape the mud from a shoe,
A knife that was little good?
And what's my hand to you?

When you were a lad at Minard
The fishing was well enough;
Your father had his boat,
Sea-eyeing, sail-winged Sireadh;
There were twenty keels afloat,
Treasure and Clan Munro.
Laughter and talk on a Monday
With all the week to go,
A lucky setting out
And the gannets high in the air,
No skipper a master
But every man his share:
Stories to tell at night
When the soft-foot women pause
To hear what their men are saying—
Stories of queer doings and of the Sight,
Of brounies and of twisted wishings,
Things sprung from a far-down cause,

Or stories of weddings and of great fishings:
And a bairn drops his playing,
Comes creeping nearer,
And the need is on him strong
To be ever minder and hearer
Of the soft sounds of the Gaelic,
At the ceilidh, in the tale and song,
In the mother's voice,
Aye coming back to him, past thought or choice,
And the summer days were long
And now, when you mind on it all,
You would liefer be living then,
When the men seemed to be free men
And the women gentle and tall,
And kinder than today,
And folk not ordered and fretting,
But the ways easy and the talk light.
Ah, Donnachadh Bàn,
The years have brought you forgetting!
You will need to mind on it right:
On the bad times, no meat and little meal,
Fear of the laird's factor,
Hate of the Big House,
Poaching when you could.
But a wild uneasy feel,
Yourself knowing the last squeal
Of the trapped rabbit in the wood.
The dreich, long Sunday,
Spider black of the Kirk
And the web of the discourse spun:
Courting, but feared of the sprung catch:
No way of escape,
No choice for another shape
To a life scarcely begun.
And when the fishing fails,
Act of God or man's act,

Poor catches and bad sales;
No altering the fact.
And never a boat at Minard
When you go there today,
And along the shore you played on
Hardly a child at play,
Nothing to be made on
Old crafts of sea or land:
Minard is dying, dying,
Carradale's turn comes next—
Unless we can deal with the sand,
Turn it and lift it,
Unless the storm will shift it
From a heavy silting and deep.
Minard might live again
If Scotland woke from her sleep.

You find, at the end's ending,
A tale already begun.
The tree had to be cut,
The promise had to be kept;
Yet nothing at all could be done
So long as Scotland slept.
But the hazel has grown the nut,
The small nut of knowledge,
In the pool waits the old salmon,
Creep nearer, oh creep,
Highlander, poacher, promiser!
The storm has shifted the sand,
Scotland stirs in her sleep,
If you look close and deep
You will see the scar on my hand,
The sign of a Highland promise,
Of a word, a light sound,
Your own promise and mine.
But the cedar lies on the ground:

Donnachadh Bàn,
Do I take the tree as a sign?

Not to me, ah not to me, to no human,
None has patience enough:
Not to your dew-pearled rose:
Only to her who is more than woman,
Alba, our mother,
Who, waiting, knows
The needs and hearts of her children,
The inner light and the stir.
As, times, I too am patient,
Finding, past shift and blur
Of a Whig-twisted history,
The things that were done to those children
And, through their pains, to her.

VII. The Green Braird of April

A maze of words in your head
For the loveliness of trees,
For the April moonshine shed
Over calm, silver-scaled seas;
But the words clamour and spread,
Senseless and bonny as birds
That you hear as you lie in your bed
And know the morning begun.
The birds sing to the sun:
I must make songs of your words.

The thoughts toss with the words,
Reaching from here and now,
Tumbling and wild like the farm birds,
The peewits over the plough:

Thoughts of Scotland and of taking courage,
How you might be if you chose
—If only a man could choose,
Choosing right, how to be and whose!—
In the kind eyes of your rose, all those
Reflected, boats set for all ports,
On all tides, all winds, wild brides;
I must make sense of your thoughts.

Ah, Donnachadh Bàn,
The catkin is off the hazel,
But it tassels light on the birk;
The braird is green on the land—
Scatter of braird on the heart!
Here for today is peace,
Though the glass runs with sand.
What shall we do with our peace?
Is there time for life to start,
Is there room to understand,
Before the hour's lease
Falls due, and there's all to face.
Hot blood and cold fact.
No choice of time or place,
But the moment come to act?

VIII. They did it

Swithering how to turn,
In a wild daze you stand,
Seeing on the one hand
Your own immediate rose
And a new song to learn.
And how would a man be bad
With the lamp lit and the welcome at night?

But your mind is torn and drawn,
Past Scotland, past the home light,
Far out to Stalingrad.
We know the look, heavy and thrawn,
Of a man wanting to die
But held in comfort and peace,
We know, your rose and I.
If they live well and die well,
Rising clean out of hell,
Is it for you to destroy
The things that mock your ease,
People, and your own life, and trees?

My soul, that country is ours,
Though the wingless sentries stand,
Skilful in peace and war:
And the fierce ramparts are manned
Against the old life and the old shame.
Surely you understand
Scotland might be the same?

Not without work, yours and mine,
Risk to the lamp-lit home,
To a life's quiet plan:
Scorn, hate, doubt of yourself,
Met with no hotter wine
Than your own heart's blood.
They did it, who began,
Lighting Iskra, the Spark,
From the same discouragement
As mine from which I write.
Yet knowing it will pass
Unhelped by dream or glass.
There were plenty risks they ran,
Fighting their own class;
They knew there could be failure,

A long return of the dark,
Death and worse for themselves:
Yet how else act as a man,
How use strength and brain?
You say there were mistakes;
We need not make them again.
Ours now to learn, not blame,
Listen—for all our sakes!
Scotland might be the same.

IX. The Gossip of Carradale

When once a thing is in print
It needs to be ten times true,
It needs to be steel and flint.
It becomes the voice of Scotland.
It stops being me and you.

The thought is clear in my mind;
But the shine goes off the salmon
As the life dries from his scales,
And the thought goes dull and blind
And the flow of the fancy fails.
The bold and exact plan
Lacks money, lacks more the man
With courage to speak and strike
As the timeous instant comes.
All I can do with a rhyme
Is to hope for a man and a time
And that like may call to like.
Where one falls out or two,
Toom tabards that drop from view,
Yet three might carry it through—

We need not always fail!—
It is nothing at all to do
With me and Donnachadh Bàn
Nor the gossip of Carradale.

I had a vision once
Of Scotland that yet may be;
Ourselves were part of it:
Me or a woman like me;
You or a man like you,
Which or who, is there a spark of matter?
It is nothing at all to do
With village snigger and chatter
Over me or Donnachadh Bàn.
I know I will be betrayed
By some that I love the best,
That maybe half loved me,
Until it came to the test
And a hard choice to be made.
I know I will be betrayed:
I think on John Maclean;
He was a highlander too,
But a better man than you,
Better than most today
In village or countryside
Or his own place, the Red Clyde,
River that bred and nursed
Broods of good lads and true:
We know the Fifty-First!
If I could make them see
Scotland that is to be,
I would work without stay or stint.
But could I be the voice of Scotland
In narrow and chilly print?

X. Fashing and Working

Day after day, fashing and working,
Lifting weights, harnessing, thinning,
Swinging engines, screwing nuts on bolts, sawing,
Against harsh weather mowing, tending and winning
Crops out of ill land in the old way, clawing
From our too well known fields,
Now at the back-end over farm boots muddying,
Hungry for slag and lime;
Pitching, loading or milking, and all the time,
Past the work's tail the mind goes studying:
Alba our mother, what have we done to thee?

Here are two wanting to marry,
Each one the other's best,
But no house in it.
What shall we do, what?
The mavie can build her nest
But not ourselves.
We can do nothing at all,
Let the fine impulse rot,
Or seek its own worst cure,
Peeking through a hole in the wall
At the Ball of Kirriemuir.
Alba our mother, what has been done to thee?

Here is a ring-net pair
Had no shot all week,
Hunting here and there
Sleepless and cold, seek
The crafty darlings, the herring:
Shot late on Thursday night,
Came in with the first light
To no buyers at Tarbert,
At Ayr, no buyers.

What will they do, what?
No time for sleep's blink nor food's snatch
Before the poor souls rot
Dead herring below the hatch—
They are needing to dump their catch,
Worse work than hauling in,
So home out of heart
With no share-out but a sore knowledge
Of social and immense sin
And their own unwilling part
In a world worse than half hungry.
Alba, our mother, what have we done to thee?

Bairns sit in our schools,
Savagely not learning,
Thinking their teachers fools,
Their thrawn minds turning
To their own four freedoms,
Freedom to smoke and drink,
To make love and earn money.
Their fathers' and mothers' way.
Who's wanting books or right play
Or who's wanting to think?
Come day, go day,
Saturday's pay-day
And out of school we go,
Get shoving it all away!
Who's wanting learning or arts?
Small need in the world they know
For the lass or lad of parts,
Toiling and moiling all hours
With never a shilling to clink,
Never lipstick nor fag
Nor the warm spark of a drink,
But for ever keeping to rules!

Ah, once we had pride and a plan
For a nation fed from her schools,
But the thing John Knox began
Is ending under our eyes.
We need another man
To shock and shake and to ding
Us to action out of surprise,
When we wake to see the thing
Complacency has allowed,
Weaving our own live bairns
Into the grip of a shroud:
Academic discipline!
Alba our mother, what did we do to thee!

I walk over my land
After a lost sheep
And a moment, tired, stand
With a look, deep, on my sad land.
After the weeks of raining
Pools of water gather
Folded in a dark hush
In the hills at the back-end;
For want of draining
Creeps in myrtle and bog-rush,
Uncropped, root and spread.
Did we think, did we intend,
Putting sheep here in the stead
Of our own hill cattle,
To spoil what we could not mend?
Alba our mother, what have we done to thee?

Sport land or holiday land
With the tourists passing through
And spending out of hand,
Is this the best we can do?
Oh beauty, oh soul, oh breath,

Is not this a way of half death?
Must we be thirled to the past
To the mist and the unused sheiling?
Over love and home and the Forty-five
Sham tunes and a sham feeling?
Must we be less than alive,
Must we lurk in a half light?
Is this the best we can do?
Or else the eager shot, the skilled cast,
And the tired stranger's delight:
Our moors to let, burns to sell,
Our Big House doors shut fast:
Although the money looks well
Is this the best we can do
For ourselves, and them, and for you?
Oh bonny one, oh crowned with living mountains,
Alba our mother, is this all we can make of thee?

Day long and night long
The thing is hurting and pressing,
Between the words of a song,
Between my washing and dressing:
When a thing is all that wrong
What I see plain before me,
Fault both of my own
And of those that got me and bore me,
Blood making trouble for bone.
But now the trouble has grown
To a giant we have to face,
And that now, in our own time and place.
Alba our mother, what must we do for thee?

XI. The Clean Blade of the Wedding

Summer hurrying Spring.
Action but nothing said
And the sheep comes clear of her fleece,
The clumsy, outworn thing,
Crawling with tick and ked,
Heavy with dirt and grease.
She is white like an idea
Coming out of a muck of words.
Lifting her half-freed head
From the grey pool of her fleece,
She is surprised and new;
For once she is beautiful.
Donnachadh Bàn,
What cleansing comes to you?

I stood at my horse's head
By the cart loaded with gravel.
You two went by in the car
As songs go by in the head:
Story of a much talked of wedding,
With plenty snigger and chatter,
The joke against the man
And worse, against the woman,
The village gossip and leer!
But the bride and the bridegroom know
The good that they have in mind
And the way they are set to go,
The clean blade of the wedding
Cutting the old life clear.
Ah, plenty cruel thoughts
But mine, mine were kind,
Standing alone in the steading,
Donnachadh Bàn!
But mine were warm with blessing
For you and Mary and Scotland.

The thing I could never do:
What was it came between?
Fear of the Big House,
Shadow of all that has been,
Class hate worse than clan,
Hate of the Big House
Sundering woman from man.
Time that old thing ends—
Ah, we could not get ending it!
The dead pain from the past
Coming between friends
And all I had hoped to do
For Scotland, and for you,
And myself, and Carradale.
I begin to understand
How I was bound to fail.
But you came again to the house
And I was sad at the dancing
With thought of all I had planned.
Donnachadh Bàn
Why did you take my hand?

Autumn hurrying summer
And too much work to do.
Sheep and cattle and harvest,
Drag and pain of the war,
No time to think on you,
No time to think on Scotland,
Nor look for a word or a sign.
Yet at least something goes right,
Though no doing of mine.
But show me a way or a light,
For my eyes are blind with work,
I am tired to my soul
And far enough from my friends,
Strayed in a pit mirk

With no guide to a goal
And no vision of ends.
So give me news of Scotland,
Of you and you and you,
Donnachadh Bàn;
The plain folk of Scotland:
What can we do?

XII. The New Song

The end of an old song
In Seventeen Seven:
The years that go by are long
And sad for Scotland
And over full of echoes
Of an old and bad song:
Disruptions and jealousies,
Small angers made to last,
And the wee folk talking big,
Beggars for favours and grants,
Boasters over the past,
And the worst in a Highland rig:
Here's to us, beggars and boasters
In the best whisky that's in it!
And a grand thing going wrong
Like the lilt of a great old song
Sung by a good singer,
But his judgment overcome
By drink and sympathy.
Better be hard and dumb
Till we hear the clear music
Of the start of a new song.

There was a man came here
Speaking to Carradale
Of a new harbour and pier.
We were all there to listen,
Hoping for grants and favours,
The tongue hanging out of the ear!
He bade us help ourselves,
We the plain folk of Scotland.
Donnachadh Bàn, did you hear
The note of a new music?
We that thought ourselves weak,
Could it be we might be strong?
Has he shown us a way to go
Though it may be rough and long?
And if we are Scots indeed
Could we make him the one we need,
This man from Kirkintilloch, this man,
Is he able for our, for Scotland's plan?
If he gives us a new song,
Have we the will to sing it?

What did he say, he,
Waking the song in our hearts?
"Scotland will only be free
With jobs and houses and health"
It is up to us to choose.
Local authorities
Have powers to plan and act
Which we must make them use:
Studying maybe at night
How best the thing's attacked,
Letters and all to write,
Checking of figure and fact:

Will we do this for Alba
If this is the service needed?

Not death, not death, but life,
The hours of a working day
And social over-time—
To clear the blood from the knife,
Maybe the only way,
Scraping away the grime
And tears of centuries
And blood of treacherous killings,
A little at a time.

We thirl ourselves to service
From a free choice and wish.
Tom Johnston said that day
To the ring-net fishermen:
"Civil servants catching fish".
How many saw what lay
Behind a phrase in a speech?
Giving up old jealousies,
Quarrels, suspicions, tricks,
And the skippers' over-reach
Of the share fishermen,
For the different ethic of service.
You too, Donnachadh Bàn,
Your trees will be Scotland too.
And we in the N.F.U.
Can surely be Alba's servants:
If all our land were Scotland's
There'd be pride in keeping her laws,
Laws of our own making!
And the pictures thronged through my head
With the strong rush and breaking
Of a long waited tide
Floating our stranded keels.
For our's the land and the water,
Ready for right possession
By men and gear and boats,

By tractors and harnessed power,
By human thought and will,
By courage to meet the hour
From the small folk here and there
Who know themselves Scots indeed
Who know they might be strong,
And it seemed he might be the man
Who could shake us surely awake and make us
Lead ourselves, thirl ourselves to a service
  known and agreed
And sing a new song.

XIII. *Work and Love*

The months and the years pass
Quickly, as good years can
For a blithe and sober man
With a daughter like a small rose
And a lamp lit in his heart.
And the anger of Scotland grows,
The need and anger of Scotland.
And I must take my part.

One man and another
Passing the sleeper, cries
Alba, Alba, Alba!
Will you stop your dreaming at last,
Wake out of a smother
Of old dreams and old lies?
As when Tom Johnston passed
Through the sleep of Carradale
And we turned uneasily.
Then back to sleep for some
But the County Council for me
With work and fighting to come.

The old scar skins over
But the shape of the cut stays,
As stays the strength of the promise,
As stand the hills of Scotland
To the end of the years and days.
And you, Donnachadh Bàn,
For her green and comely veil,
Have planned and planted a forest.
And myself, the laird and writer,
Neither did I fail
Over building of roads and houses
And a harbour for Carradale.
And each looks to the other
For the heart-word of praise.
It is work and love for the mending
Of an often broken promise:
After ill and false intending
Of all the centuries past,
Faith between Highlands and Lowlands.

At last and at long last
There will be getting and spending
For the sake of Alba, our mother,
There will be hope and life,
The pibroch over the hill
And the fiery cross of good will,
And I see my poem's ending
And the cleansing of the knife.